Beloved Baby™

A Baby's Scrapbook and Journal

By Michaela Angela Davis

With Illustrations & Design by Lesley Ehlers

POCKET BOOKS

New York   London   Toronto   Sydney   Tokyo   Singapore

POCKET BOOKS, a division of Simon & Schuster Inc.
1230 Avenue of the Americas, New York, N.Y. 10020

ISBN 0-671-52269-8

First Pocket Books hardcover printing May 1995

10 9 8 7 6 5 4 3 2 1

POCKET and colophon are registered trademarks of Simon & Schuster Inc.

Printed in the U.S.A.

Dear Beloved Baby,
        May you love and be loved
your entire life as purely
and freely as you are
at this wondrous moment.

Many Loving Hands

I have had many wonderful experiences in my life, yet my journey in parenting has been one full of wonder. Each step, each gesture, each new idea, fills me with awe and joy.

As each child is unique, so is the journey, so is the parenting. This scrapbook has been created to preserve your moments of wonder.

There are "coaching" questions for each section, yet feel free to feel free. There are no rules. This is not a quiz, this is your child's special journey. So, go on and include all the voices, all the pictures, all the memories, and all the magic.

It has been said that a child is born into a tribe, a village, a community. It takes many people to raise a healthy, happy child. It takes a lot of love and many hands. This book is for those people.

But most important, this book is for the beloved baby. What a gift, to see how well you were loved as a baby! As these miracles are gathered and recorded in the beginning of life, it is my hope that the beloved baby, family and friends will continue to discover magic throughout the entire wondrous journey.

Peace,
Michaela Angela Davis

Mommy and Me

*Place photo of mommy in her pregnancy
or photo of mommy and baby here*

My Picture in My Mommy

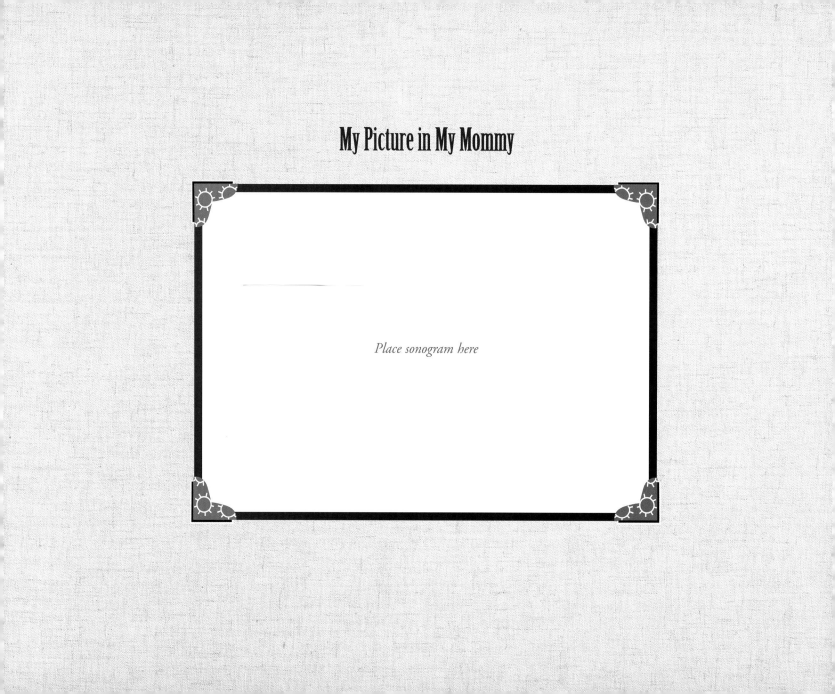

Place sonogram here

My Name

My name, _____ ,
is the title to my life's glorious song.
Let me sing it with the angels all day long.

_____

_____

_____

_____

_____

_____

_____

_____

meaning of my name • what language it is from • whom or what I am named after
who chose it • why

My First Day

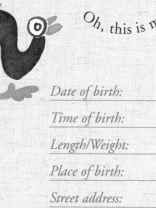

Date of birth: _____

Time of birth: _____

Length/Weight: _____

Place of birth: _____

Street address: _____

Delivered by: _____

Something special to note: _____

_____

_____

_____

My First Day

Let us sing and shout!

Who came to see me:

_____

_____

_____

_____

The weather:

_____

_____

Other news of the day:

_____

_____

_____

_____

I am wrapped in a blanket of light, and there are angels all about.

Parent

_____

Grandparents

_____

_____

My Roots

I am one with the earth, I reach for the sky...

Great Grandparents _____   Great Grandparents

_____   _____

_____   _____

Great Great Grandparents   Great Great Grandparents   Great Great Grandparents   Great Great Grandparents

_____   _____   _____   _____

_____   _____

Parent

_____

Grandparents

_____

_____

My ancestral roots give me strength to climb high.

My Roots

Great Grandparents

_____

_____

Great Grandparents

_____

_____

Great Great Grandparents

_____

_____

Great Great Grandparents

_____

_____

Great Great Grandparents

_____

_____

Great Great Grandparents

_____

_____

My Parents

My Parents

Place photo of parent here

Place photo of parent here

My Family

_____

_____

_____

_____

_____

_____

_____

_____

_____

_____

_____

people in my life • names • ages • where they live • relationship to me

My beloved family, I thank you for all your love and care…

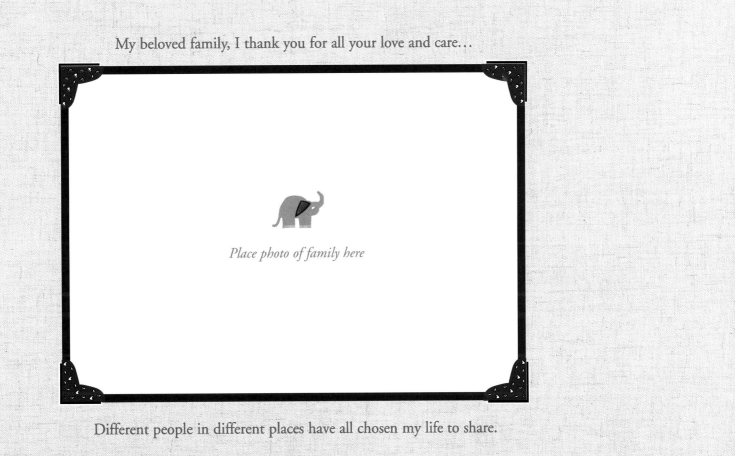

Place photo of family here

Different people in different places have all chosen my life to share.

My Gifts

baby gifts • who gave them • how I played with them

My Welcoming

I am here! I am here!
Sing it loud! Sing it strong!
I join the ancestors in my welcoming song.

_____

_____

_____

_____

_____

_____

_____

_____

_____

_____

a party · a christening · a baptism · a bris · when · where · who led · who came
other details: food, music, special clothing, etc. · or photo

My Stars

Sun sign: _____

What it means: _____

_____

_____

_____

Other astrological signs: _____

What they mean: _____

_____

_____

attach the horoscope of the day

My Family's Spiritual Journey

My spirit is my power. I am divinely guided—every day and every hour.

_____

_____

_____

_____

_____

_____

_____

_____

_____

_____

religion · philosophy · ceremonies · rituals

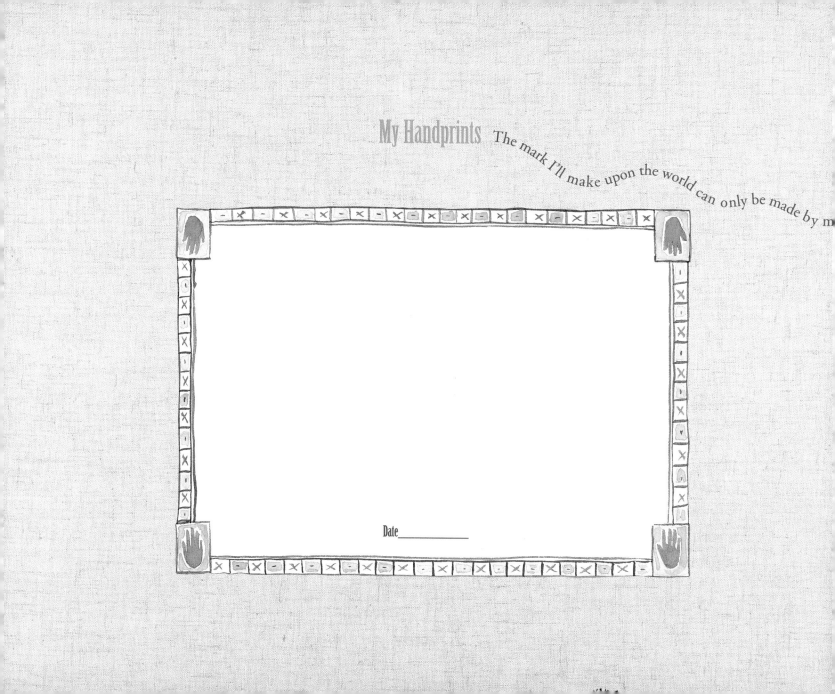

My Handprints

The mark I'll make upon the world can only be made by m

Date_____

My Footprints

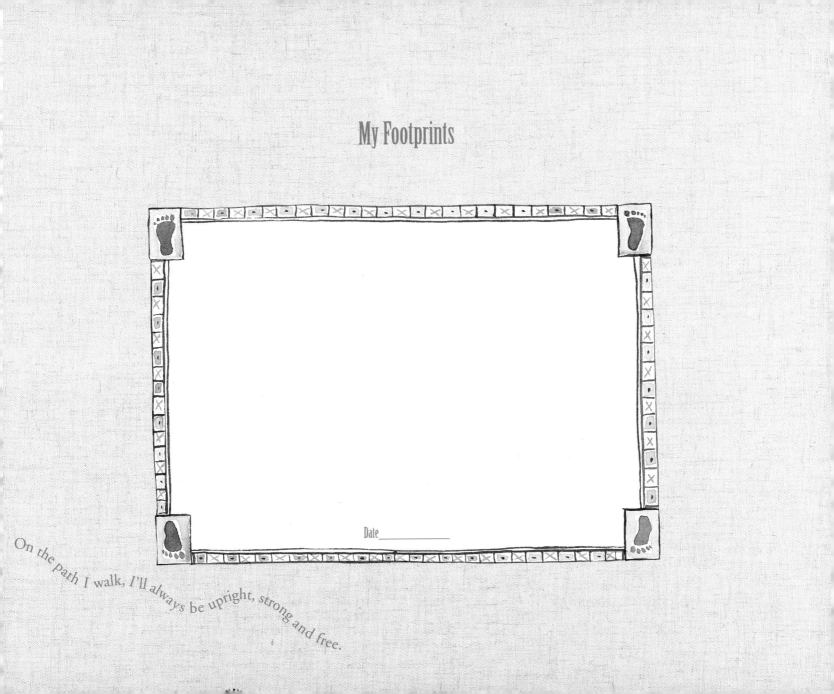

Date_____

On the path I walk, I'll always be upright, strong and free.

My Hair

My hair is my choice. It is tame. It is free. It is precious and beautiful, just like me!

Here is a lock of my hair. A flower picked from a unique and beautiful garden.

color · favorite style · family similarity · photo

My Familiar

I have something special
that was chosen just for me.
It brings me joy and comfort,
and keeps me company.

what it is: animal, doll, etc. • who chose it • my name for it

My Visits to the Doctor

Date: _____

Purpose: _____

Doctor's name: _____

Shots: _____

Weight: _____ Length: _____

Head size: _____

Date: _____

Purpose: _____

Doctor's name: _____

Shots: _____

Weight: _____ Length: _____

Head size: _____

Date: _____

Purpose: _____

Doctor's name: _____

Shots: _____

Weight: _____ Length: _____

Head size: _____

Date: _____

Purpose: _____

Doctor's name: _____

Shots: _____

Weight: _____ Length: _____

Head size: _____

My First Tooth

Date:

Date:

Purpose:

Doctor's name:

Shots:

Weight: Length:

Head size:

Date:

Purpose:

Doctor's name:

Shots:

Weight: Length:

Head size:

Date:

Purpose:

Doctor's name:

Shots:

Weight: Length:

Head size:

Date:

Purpose:

Doctor's name:

Shots:

Weight: Length:

Head size:

My Growing Independence

I am growing. I am glowing. I am spinning. I am winning.
I am prancing. I am dancing…

First sleep through the night:

_____

_____

First roll over:

_____

_____

First sit-up:

_____

_____

First crawl:

_____

_____

First walk:

_____

_____

I am happy to be flowering into me.

First wave: _____

_____

First potty: _____

_____

Note other important milestones: _____

_____

_____

_____

_____

My Expressions

My eyes open wide like the morning sun,
My smile twinkles like stars when night has begun.

_____

_____

_____

_____

_____

_____

_____

_____

_____

favorite grimaces, sounds, giggles, squeals, gurgles, etc.
what and who causes them • family similarity

Place photo of my best expression here.

My Words

My words are alive. I'll speak with truth and care. Let love and understanding be what I choose to share.

first words • when and to whom • favorite words • funny or made-up words

My Feelings

I tingle and bubble with laughs and cries. I set free what's happening inside.

_____

_____

_____

_____

_____

_____

_____

_____

_____

general disposition • who • and what makes me angry, joyful, excited, calm, etc.

My Music

There is music all around me.

Melodies dance through the air.

A favorite song, a special instrument

that I can play anywhere.

favorite lullaby, song, or music
my special instrument: a rattle, a drum, a pot and a spoon, etc.

My Stories

favorite stories • who told them • whether made up or from books, movies, etc.

My Favorite Things

what they are ▪ where they came from

My Games

Ooh, I can play, I can play! I jump through rings of light and sing giggles all day.

favorite games • whom I played with

My Books

Rejoice in the magic that books bring. In stories,
anything can happen: fish walk about, and elephants sing!

favorite titles • who gave them to me • who read them with me • favorite characters

My Talents

new skills: identifying objects, stacking blocks, fitting objects together, etc. • dates

My Adventure

I love to walk, ride and fly. With my head held high,
I watch the clouds roll by.

_____

_____

_____

_____

_____

_____

_____

_____

_____

_____

a special outing, a vacation, etc. • favorite park/zoo • when and with whom

My First Celebration

christmas, kwanzaa, ramadan, hanukah, family gathering, etc.
who was there • how we celebrated

My World

My world is filled with darkness and light.
May I always seek what is peaceful and right.

Popular music/songs: _____
_____
_____
_____

Fashion trends: _____
_____
_____
_____

Television and movie hits: _____
_____
_____

Slang and expressions of the day:

_____
_____
_____
_____
_____

News events:

_____
_____
_____
_____
_____

My Play Names

I have some names that are different from my own:
cute names, silly names ... names that tickle my funny bone!

nicknames and other terms of endearment • who gave them to me • why

My Special Names for People

friends, sitters, teachers, people in my community • our activities together

My First Birthday

who celebrated with me • gifts • food • music • baby's reaction

Here is the first birthday picture of me.
May I always see myself beautiful, pure and free!

Place photo of celebration here.

My Very Special People

Many loving hands take good care of me.
I'm healthy and happy, thanks to my extended family.

My Special People's Thoughts for Me

Name/Address:

_____

_____

Date/Message:

_____

_____

_____

_____

_____

_____

_____

_____

My Special People's Thoughts for Me

Name/Address:
_____
_____

Date/Message:
_____
_____
_____
_____
_____
_____

My Special People's Thoughts for Me

Name/Address:
_____
_____

Date/Message:
_____
_____
_____
_____
_____
_____
_____

My Special People's Thoughts for Me

Name/Address: _____

_____

Date/Message: _____

_____

_____

_____

_____

_____

My Special People's Thoughts for Me

Name/Address:

Date/Message:

Save forever the magic moments,
the precious pictures, the wondrous words,
the living love.
Keep here the true treasures of life
and always remember the beauty of birth.

I grow in beauty every day. The world opens wide to me as I learn, dream and play.